CALIFORNIA JOURNEYS

Houghton
Mifflin
Harcourt

Program Consultants

Shervaughnna Anderson · Marty Hougen
Carol Jago · Erik Palmer · Shane Templeton
Sheila Valencia · MaryEllen Vogt

Consulting Author · Irene Fountas

Cover illustration by Scott Nash.

Copyright © 2017 by Houghton Mifflin Harcourt Publishing Company

Printed in the U.S.A.

ISBN 978-0-544-54394-2

2 3 4 5 6 7 8 9 10 0868 23 22 21 20 19 18 17 16 15
4500545657   A B C D E F G

Unit 1

Unit 2

Unit 3

6

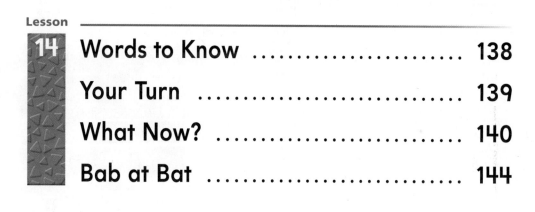

Lesson

1

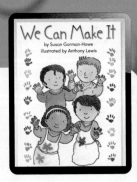

WORDS TO KNOW

High-Frequency Words

I

Vocabulary Reader

Context Cards

ELA RI.K.1, RF.K.3c, SL.K.2 **ELD** ELD.PI.K.1, ELD.PI.K.3

Words to Know

Read Together

▸ Read the word.

▸ Talk about the picture.

I

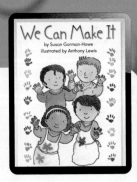

I have a big family!

Your Turn

Talk About It!

What Makes
a Family?

Families are different.   What
is the same about all families?
Share ideas with a partner.

See What We Can Do

by Susan Gorman-Howe

illustrated by Sue Dennen

We Can Make It

by Susan Gorman-Howe

illustrated by Anthony Lewis

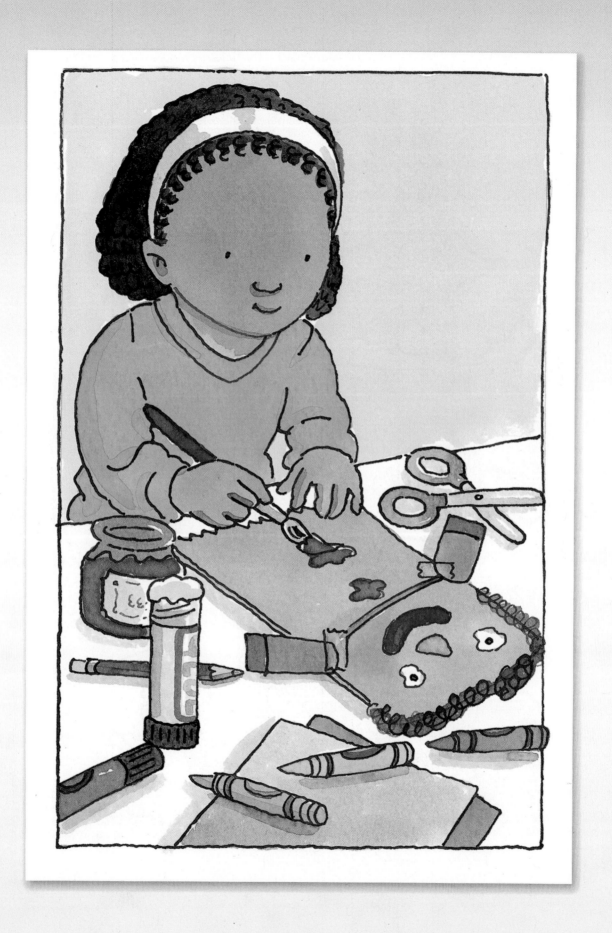

We Go to School
by Susan Gorman-Howe
illustrated by Maryann Cocca-Leffler

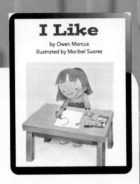

I Like
by Owen Marcus
illustrated by Maribel Suarez

WORDS TO KNOW
High-Frequency Words

like

Vocabulary Reader

At School
by Philip Rush

HOUGHTON MIFFLIN

Context Cards

We like to go to school!

How Do I Use It?
Pam and Jamal like to draw. Do you
like ice cream?

Talk It Over:
Think about things you like. Take turns talking
about them with a partner.

ELA RL.K.1, RF.K.3c, SL.K.2 **ELD** ELD.PI.K.1, ELD.PI.K.3

Words to Know

Read Together

▸ Read the word.

▸ Talk about the picture.

like

We like to go to school!

Your Turn

Talk About It!

Talk about what happens when the dinosaurs do not follow the rules. Why do we have rules at school?

We Go to School

by Susan Gorman-Howe

illustrated by Maryann Cocca-Leffler

I Like

by Owen Marcus

illustrated by Maribel Suarez

I like .

I like .

I like .

I like  .

Baby Bear's Family
by Susan Gorman-Howe
illustrated by Angela Jarecki

The Party
by Ron Kingsley
illustrated by Yvette Banek

WORDS TO KNOW

High-Frequency Words

the

Vocabulary Reader

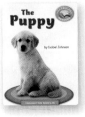
The Puppy
by Isabel Johnson

Context Cards

Do you see the puppy?

ELA RL.K.3, RF.K.3c, SL.K.2 ELD ELD.PI.K.1, ELD.PI.K.3

Words to Know

(Read Together)

▶ Read the word.

▶ Talk about the picture.

the

Do you see the puppy?

Your Turn

Talk About It!

Talk to a friend. Tell why pets need someone to take care of them.

Baby Bear's Family

by Susan Gorman-Howe

illustrated by Angela Jarecki

The Party

by Ron Kingsley

illustrated by Yvette Banek

I like the .

I like the 🎁.

I like the .

I like the .

WORDS TO KNOW

High-Frequency Words

and

Vocabulary Reader

Context Cards

ELA RI.K.3, RF.K.3c, SL.K.2 ELD ELD.PI.K.1

Words to Know

Read Together

▸ Read the word.

▸ Talk about the picture.

and

A worker has a saw and a hammer.

Your Turn

Talk About It!

What kinds of work do people do? Tell a partner.

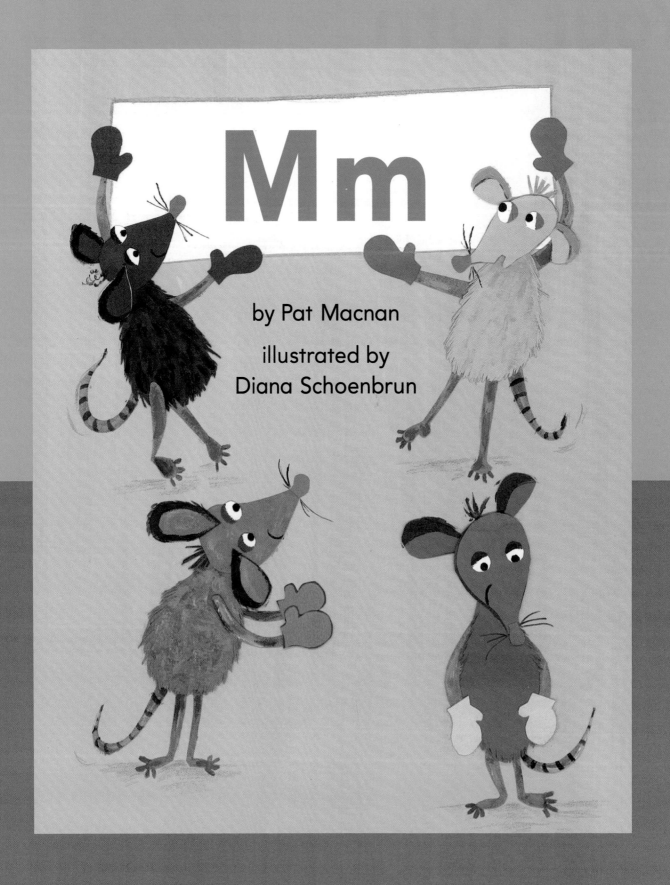

Mm

by Pat Macnan

illustrated by
Diana Schoenbrun

Mm

I Like Mm

by Pat Macnan

I like the .

I like the .

I like the .

Mm

I like the 🥛 and the 🧁🧁.

Lesson 5

WORDS TO KNOW

High-Frequency Words

I
like

Vocabulary Reader

Context Cards

ELA RI.K.7, RF.K.3c, SL.K.2
ELD ELD.PI.K.1, ELD PI.K.11, ELD.PII.K.3a

48

Words to Know

Read Together

▶ You learned these words. Use each one in a sentence.

I

I have a big family!

like

We like to go to school!

Your Turn

Talk About It!

The Handiest Things
in the World
ANDREW CLEMENTS
Photographs by Raquel Jaramillo

How do tools help us do
things with our hands?
Tell a partner what you think.

Ss

by Pat Macnan

illustrated by Diana Schoenbrun

I Like Ss

by Pablo Lopez

I like the .

Ss

I like the .

Ss

I like the ☀.

Ss

I like the 🥛 and the 🥪.

WORDS TO KNOW

High-Frequency Words

see

Vocabulary
Reader

Context
Cards

ELA RI.K.1, RF.K.3c, SL.K.2 ELD ELD.PI.K.1, ELD.PI.K.3

Words to Know

Read Together

▸ Read the word.

▸ Talk about the picture.

see

What can you see in the city?

Your Turn

Talk About It!

How do you use your senses to learn about the world? Tell a friend.

Aa

by Roberto Livingston

illustrated by Bernard Adnet

Aa

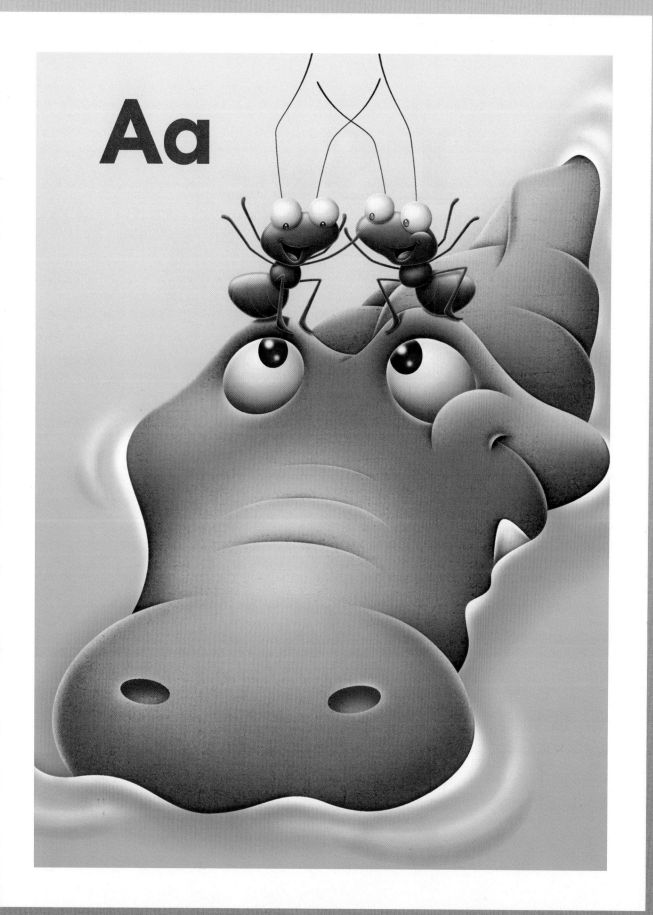

I See

by Sheila Hoffman

I see the .

Aa

I see the .

Aa

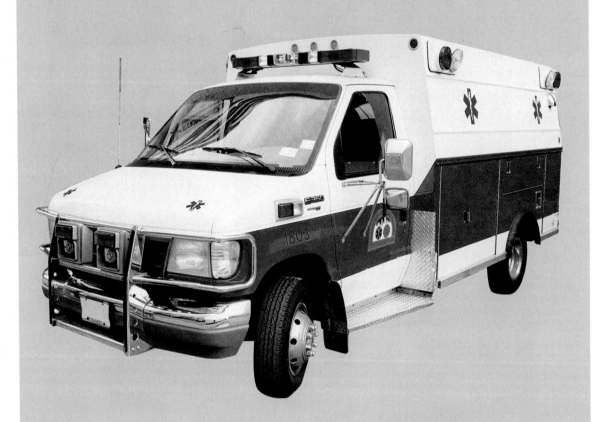

I see the .

Aa

I see the  .

Tt
by Nimesh Sing
illustrated by Priscilla Burris

We Like Toys
by Matthew Lorer

WORDS TO KNOW
High-Frequency Words

we

Vocabulary Reader

On the Farm
by Alex Corro

Context Cards

Our cat purrs when **we** pet her.

ELA RL.K.1, RF.K.3c **ELD** ELD.PI.K.1

Words to Know

Read Together

▸ Read the word.

▸ Talk about the picture.

we

Our cat purrs when **we** pet her.

Your Turn

Talk About It!

How do people and animals communicate? Talk about it with a friend. Use words from the **Big Book** as you share ideas.

Tt

by Nimesh Sing
illustrated by Priscilla Burris

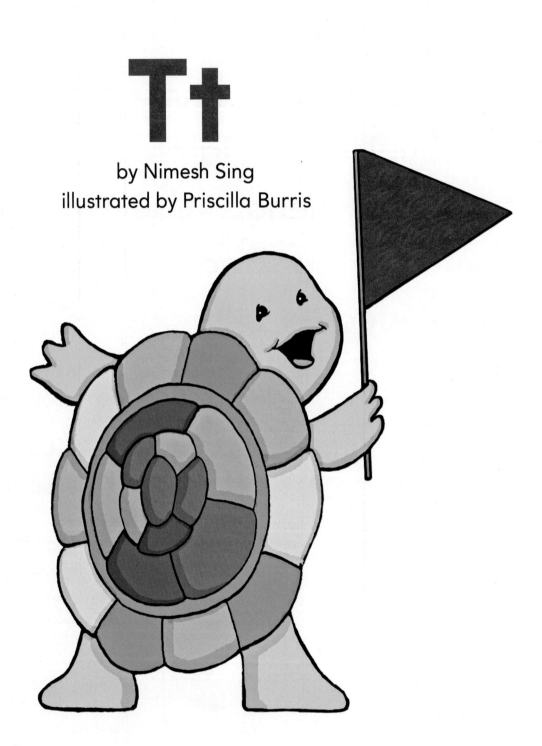

Tt

We Like Toys

by Matthew Lorer

Tt

I like the .

Tt

We like the 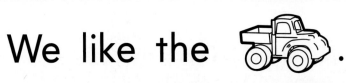.

Tt

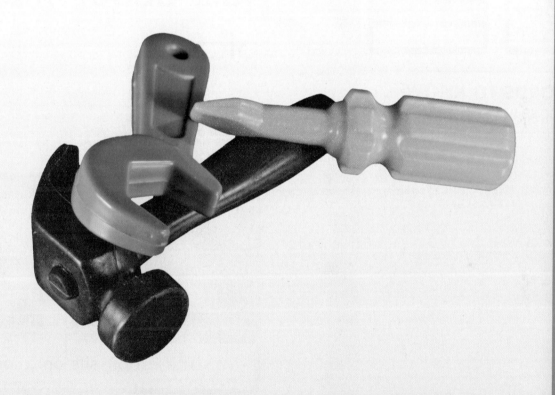

We like the 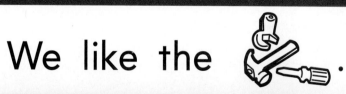 .

Words to Know

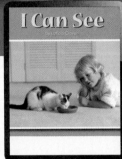

WORDS TO KNOW

High-Frequency Words

a

▸ Read the word.

▸ Talk about the picture.

Vocabulary Reader

Context Cards

a

This rabbit sits on a log.

Your Turn

Talk About It!

Why do different animals move in different ways? Talk about it with a friend.

Cc

by David Ashford

illustrated by John Segal

Cc

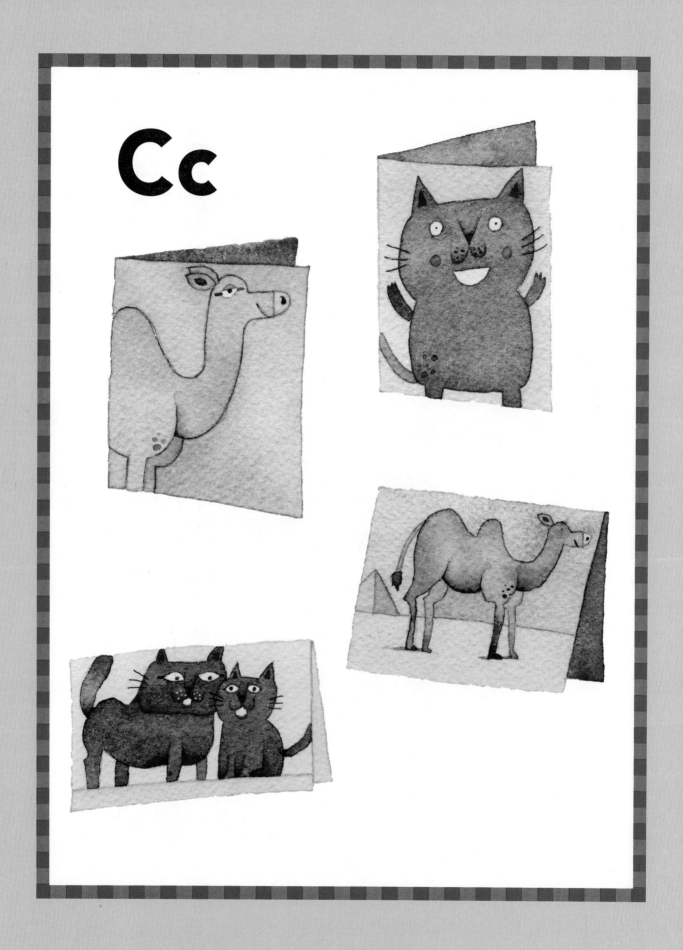

I Can See

by Laticia Craven

I see a .

Cc

I see a .

Cc

I see a  .

Cc

I see a .

Lesson

9

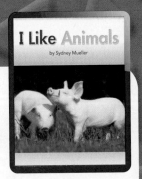

WORDS TO KNOW
High-Frequency Words

to

Vocabulary Reader

Context Cards

ELA RI.K.7, RF.K.3c, SL.K.2 **ELD** ELD.PI.K.1, ELD.PI.K.3

Words to Know

Read Together

▶ Read the word.

▶ Talk about the picture.

to

We like **to** ride our bikes!

Your Turn

Talk About It!

Why do people use wheels?
Talk with a partner.

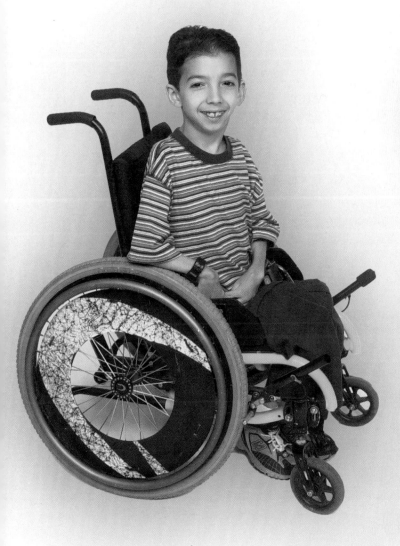

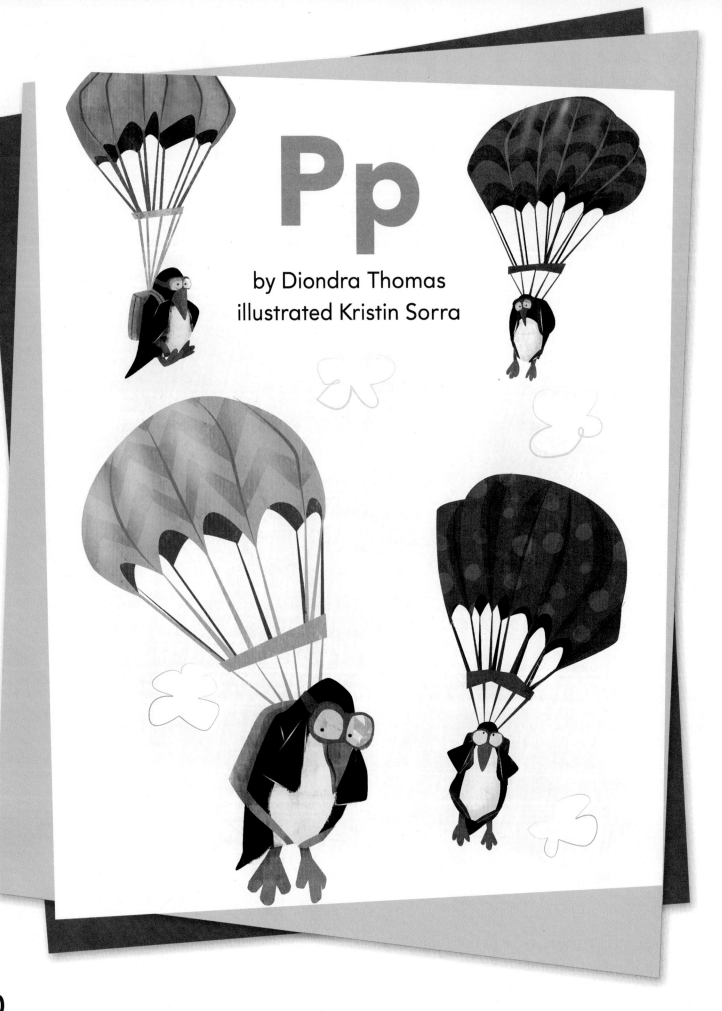

P p

by Diondra Thomas
illustrated Kristin Sorra

Pp

I Like Animals

by Sydney Mueller

I like to see 🐖🐖.

Pp

I like to see .

Pp

I like to see  .

Pp

I like to see 🦜🦜 .

Mmmm, Good!
by Angela Ferie
illustrated Ana Ochoa

The Playground
by Paul Falcon
illustrated by Robin Oz

WORDS TO KNOW
High-Frequency Words

see

we

Vocabulary Reader

Our Classroom
by Jeka Hubert

Context Cards

ELA RL.K.1, RL.K.3, RF.K.3c ELD ELD.PI.K.1, ELD.PII.K.3a

Words Read Together to Know

▶ You learned these words. Use each one in a sentence.

see

What can you see in the city?

we

Our cat purrs when we pet her.

Your Turn

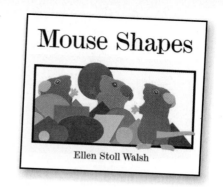

Mouse Shapes

Ellen Stoll Walsh

Talk About It!

What do the mice make with shapes in the **Big Book?** What can we create with shapes? Talk with a partner.

Mmmm, Good!

by Angela Ferie
illustrated Ana Ochoa

I see .

I like .

We like  .

102

We like to see .

The Playground

by Paul Falcon

illustrated by Robin Oz

I like the .

I like to  .

We see the  .

We like the .

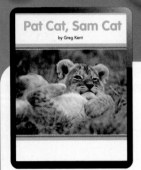

Pat Cat, Sam Cat
by Greg Kent

Pam Cat
by Louise Andreas
illustrated by Judith Lanfredi

WORDS TO KNOW

High-Frequency Words

come

me

Vocabulary
Reader

Context
Cards

Fun in July
by Zachary Lambert

The rain will come down in spring.

ELA RI.K.1, RI.K.10, RF.K.3c ELD ELD.PI.K.1

Words to Know

Read Together

▸ Read the words.

▸ Talk about the pictures.

come

1

The rain will come down in spring.

me

2

This hat is for me.

Your Turn

Talk About It!

How does the weather change in different months and seasons? Talk to a friend about it.

Pat Cat, Sam Cat

by Greg Kent

Pat Cat, Pat Cat.

I am Pat Cat.

Come to me, Pat Cat!
Pat Cat sat.

Sam Cat, Sam Cat.
I am Sam Cat.

Come to me, Sam Cat!
Sam Cat sat.

Pam Cat

by Louise Andreas
illustrated by Judith Lanfredi

Pam Cat! Pam Cat! Pam Cat!
Pam Cat! Pam Cat! Pam Cat!

I see Pam Cat.
Come to me, Pam Cat.

Pam Cat sat.

Pam Cat and I sat.

I pat Pam Cat.

I pat and pat Pam Cat.

I Can Nap
by Christopher Lawrence

Tap with Me
by Cara Blanco
illustrated by Holli Conger

WORDS TO KNOW
High-Frequency Words

with
my

Vocabulary Reader

Animals in the Snow

Context Cards

ELA RL.K.1, RF.K.3c   ELD ELD.PI.K1

Words to Know

Read Together

▸ Read the words.

▸ Talk about the pictures.

with

The trees are covered with snow.

my

The snowman wears my scarf.

Your Turn

Talk About It!

snow

Manya Stojic

What do animals do when the weather changes? Talk to a partner about it.

I Can Nap

by Christopher Lawrence

🐻 can nap.

🐻 can nap, nap, nap, nap.

I am Dan.

I can nap with my .

We can nap, nap, nap, nap.

 can nap.

 can nap, nap, nap, nap.

I am Pat.

I can nap with my .

We can nap, nap, nap, nap.

Tap with Me

by Cara Blanco

illustrated by Holli Conger

I can tap.
I tap, tap, tap.

I can tap. Nan can tap.
Nan can tap, tap, tap.

I can tap with Nan.
Tap, tap, tap.

I am Tap Man!
Tap, tap, tap! Tap Man!

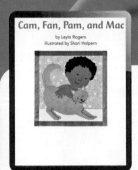

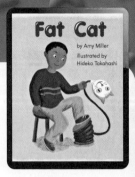

WORDS TO KNOW
High-Frequency Words

you
what

Vocabulary Reader

Context Cards

ELA RI.K.1, RF.K.3c, SL.K.1a ELD ELD.PI.K.1

Words to Know

Read Together

▸ Read the words.

▸ Talk about the pictures.

you

Do you see the butterfly?

what

What colors do you see?

Your Turn

Talk About It!

What Do You Do With a Tail Like This?

Steve Jenkins & Robin Page

How do animals use their body parts? Talk to a partner about it.

Cam, Fan, Pam, and Mac

by Leyla Rogers

illustrated by Shari Halpern

Cam can see a tan cat.

Cam can pat the tan cat.

The fat tan cat can see Cam.

Fan can see Nat.
Can Nat see Fan?
Nat can! Nat can!

Pam can see Sam.

Sam can nap, nap, nap!

Pam sat with Sam.

What can Mac see?
Mac can see you.

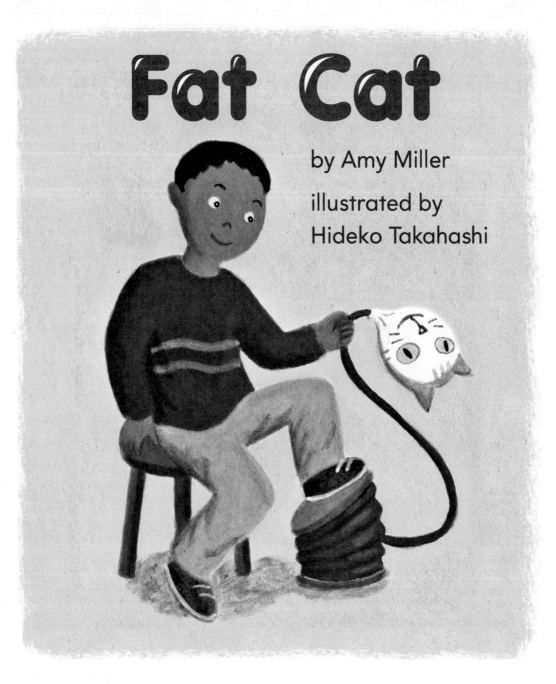

Fat Cat

by Amy Miller

illustrated by
Hideko Takahashi

Sam sat.

Sam sat to tap, tap, tap.

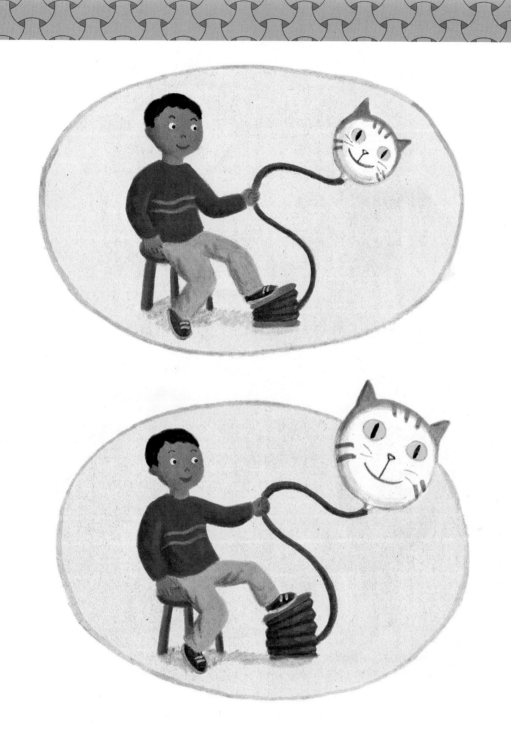

Can you see the cat?
Sam can tap, tap, tap, tap.

Tap, Sam! Tap, Sam!
Tap. Tap. Tap.

Can you see the fat cat?
What a fat, fat cat!

What Now?
by Suzanne Gerardi

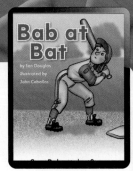
Bab at Bat
by Ian Douglas
illustrated by
John Ceballos

WORDS TO KNOW

High-Frequency Words

are

now

Vocabulary Reader

Context Cards

ELA RF.K.3c, SL.K.2 ELD ELD.PI.K.1

Words to Know

Read Together

▸ Read the words.

▸ Talk about the pictures.

are

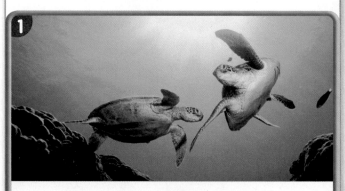

1

The turtles are swimming.

now

2

The turtle is sleeping now.

Your Turn

Talk About It!

What animals can you find near a pond? Talk to a partner about it.

What Now?
by Suzanne Gerardi

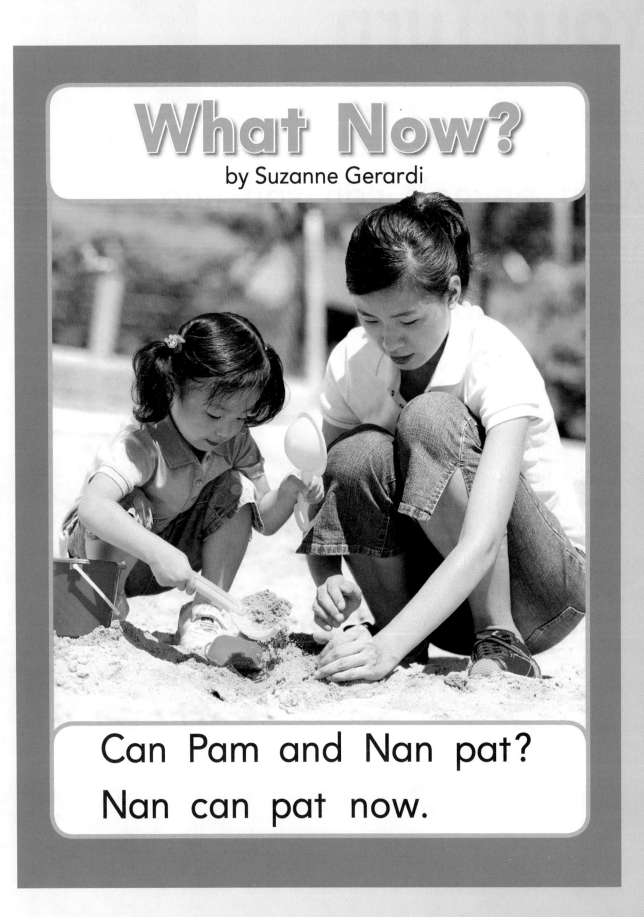

Can Pam and Nan pat?
Nan can pat now.

Can Nat tap? Nat can!
Nat can tap now.

Sam and Bab are at bat.
Can Sam bat? Sam can.
Bat, Sam, bat!

Now we can nap.

Bab at Bat

by Ian Douglas

illustrated by

John Ceballos

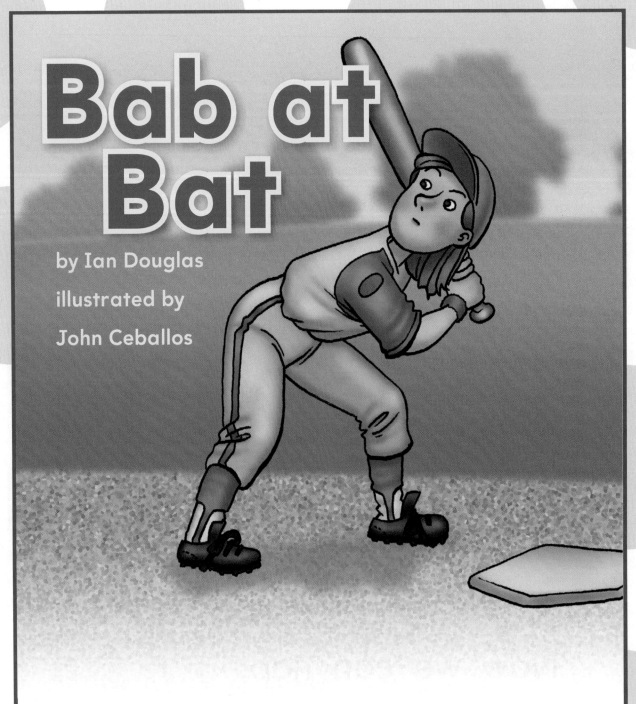

See Bab at bat?
Bab can bat.

Bab can bat now.
Bat, Bab! Bat!
Bam!

Bab CAN bat!
Pat can see Bab bat.
You can, Pat! You can!

Pat can. We can.
We are , Pat!

WORDS TO KNOW

High-Frequency Words

come

me

Vocabulary Reader

Context Cards

In the Sky

ELA RI.K.1, RI.K.2, RF.K.3c ELD ELD.PI.K.1

Words to Know

Read Together

▶ You learned these words. Use each one in a sentence.

come

The rain will come down in spring.

me

This hat is for me.

Your Turn

Talk About It!

What can we see in the sky? Talk to a friend about it.

Mac and Pam Cat

by Nina Dimopolous
illustrated by Bari Weissmann

Mac sat and sat.

Pam Cat sat.

Mac can pat Pam Cat.

Mac sat with Pam Cat.
Mac can fan Pam Cat.

Come to me, Pam Cat.
Pam Cat! Pam Cat!

Come with Me

by Roger DiPaulo

illustrated by Fahimeh Amiri

Nat sat and sat.
Nat sat, sat, sat.

Come with me, Bab!
Bab! Bab! Bab!

Nat sat. Bab sat.
Nat can see Nan.
Bab can see Nan.

Nat sat. Bab sat. Nan sat.

Word Lists

Unit 1

1

See What We Can Do	We Can Make It
Wordless Story	Wordless Story

2

We Go to School	I Like
Wordless Story	High-Frequency Words
	I, like

3

Baby Bear's Family	The Party
Wordless Story	High-Frequency Words
	I, like, the

4

Mm	I Like Mm	
Suggested Words	Suggested Words	High-Frequency Words
masks, mice, mittens, moon, mountains, mouse, music	milk, moon, mouse, muffins	and, I, like, the

Lesson	Ss	I Like Ss	
5	Suggested Words	Suggested Words	High-Frequency Words
	sailboat, sailing, sailor, sea, seal, soccer, sun, surf, surfboard	sailboat, sandwich, seal, soup, sun	and, I, like, the

Unit 2

Lesson	Aa	I See	
6	Suggested Words	Suggested Words	High-Frequency Words
	acrobats, alligator, anthill, ants, apple	ambulance, ants, apple, astronaut	I, see, the

Lesson	Tt	We Like Toys	
7	Suggested Words	Suggested Words	High-Frequency Words
	teddy bear, tracks, train, triangle, trampolines, tree, turtle, turtles	tiger, tools, toys, truck, twins	I, like, the, we

Lesson	Cc	I Can See	
8	Suggested Words	Suggested Words	High-Frequency Words
	camel, camels, cap, carrots, cars, castle, cat, cats, clouds, computer	castle, cat, caterpillar, computer	a, I, see

Lesson 9

Pp	I Like Animals	
Suggested Words	**Suggested Words**	**High-Frequency Words**
pajamas, pan, parachutes, pencils, penguins, pirouettes, pop, popcorn	pandas, parrots, pigs, polar bears	I, like, see, to

Lesson 10

Mmmm, Good!		The Playground	
Suggested Words	**High-Frequency Words**	**Suggested Words**	**High-Frequency Words**
apples, carrots, pumpkins, tomatoes	I, like, see, to, we	jump rope, slide, sprinkler, swings, water fountain	I, like, see, the, to, we

Unit 3

Lesson 11

Pat Cat, Sam Cat		Pam Cat	
Decodable Words	**High-Frequency Words**	**Decodable Words**	**High-Frequency Words**
Target Skill: Words with Short *a* am*, cat, Pat, Sam, sat	come, I, me, to	Target Skill: Words with Short *a* cat, Pam, pat, sat	and, come, I, me, see, to

Lesson 12

I Can Nap		Tap with Me	
Decodable Words	**High-Frequency Words**	**Decodable Words**	**High-Frequency Words**
Target Skill: Words with *n* am*, can*, Dan, nap, Pat	I, my, with, we	Target Skill: Words with *n* am*, can*, man*, Nan, tap	I, me, with

160

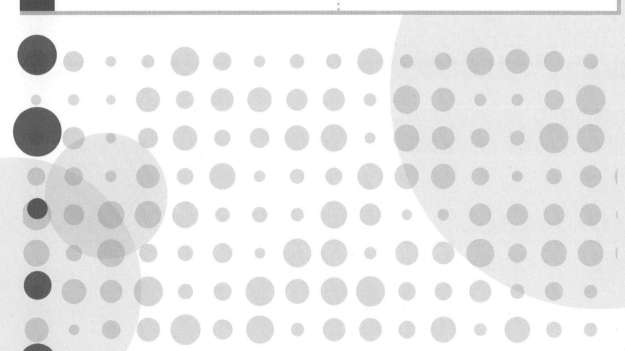

Photo Credits

California Common Core State Standards for English Language Arts

LITERATURE	
Key Ideas and Details	
RL.K.1	With prompting and support, ask and answer questions about key details in a text.
RL.K.2	With prompting and support, retell familiar stories, including key details.
RL.K.3	With prompting and support, identify characters, settings, and major events in a story.
Craft and Structure	
RL.K.4	Ask and answer questions about unknown words in a text. **(See grade K Language standards 4–6 for additional expectations.) CA**
RL.K.5	Recognize common types of texts (e.g., storybooks, poems, **fantasy, realistic text). CA**
RL.K.6	With prompting and support, name the author and illustrator of a story and define the role of each in telling the story.
Integration of Knowledge and Ideas	
RL.K.7	With prompting and support, describe the relationship between illustrations and the story in which they appear (e.g., what moment in a story an illustration depicts).
RL.K.8	(Not applicable to literature)
RL.K.9	With prompting and support, compare and contrast the adventures and experiences of characters in familiar stories.
Range of Reading and Level of Text Complexity	
RL.K.10a	Actively engage in group reading activities with purpose and understanding. **Activate prior knowledge related to the information and events in texts. CA**
RL.K.10b	Actively engage in group reading activities with purpose and understanding. **Use illustrations and context to make predictions about text. CA**
INFORMATIONAL TEXT	
Key Ideas and Details	
RI.K.1	With prompting and support, ask and answer questions about key details in a text.
RI.K.2	With prompting and support, identify the main topic and retell key details of a text.
RI.K.3	With prompting and support, describe the connection between two individuals, events, ideas, or pieces of information in a text.
Craft and Structure	
RI.K.4	With prompting and support, ask and answer questions about unknown words in a text. **(See grade K Language standards 4–6 for additional expectations.) CA**
RI.K.5	Identify the front cover, back cover, and title page of a book.
RI.K.6	Name the author and illustrator of a text and define the role of each in presenting the ideas or information in a text.

Integration of Knowledge and Ideas	
RI.K.7	With prompting and support, describe the relationship between illustrations and the text in which they appear (e.g., what person, place, thing, or idea in the text an illustration depicts).
RI.K.8	With prompting and support, identify the reasons an author gives to support points in a text.
RI.K.9	With prompting and support, identify basic similarities in and differences between two texts on the same topic (e.g., in illustrations, descriptions, or procedures).
Range of Reading and Level of Text Complexity	
RI.K.10a	Actively engage in group reading activities with purpose and understanding. **Activate prior knowledge related to the information and events in texts. CA**
RI.K.10b	Actively engage in group reading activities with purpose and understanding. **Use illustrations and context to make predictions about text. CA**

FOUNDATIONAL SKILLS

Print Concepts	
RF.K.1a	Demonstrate understanding of the organization and basic features of print. Follow words from left to right, top to bottom, and page by page.
RF.K.1b	Demonstrate understanding of the organization and basic features of print. Recognize that spoken words are represented in written language by specific sequences of letters.
RF.K.1c	Demonstrate understanding of the organization and basic features of print. Understand that words are separated by spaces in print.
RF.K.1d	Demonstrate understanding of the organization and basic features of print. Recognize and name all upper- and lowercase letters of the alphabet.
Phonological Awareness	
RF.K.2a	Demonstrate understanding of spoken words, syllables, and sounds (phonemes). Recognize and produce rhyming words.
RF.K.2b	Demonstrate understanding of spoken words, syllables, and sounds (phonemes). Count, pronounce, blend, and segment syllables in spoken words.
RF.K.2c	Demonstrate understanding of spoken words, syllables, and sounds (phonemes). Blend and segment onsets and rimes of single-syllable spoken words.
RF.K.2d	Demonstrate understanding of spoken words, syllables, and sounds (phonemes). Isolate and pronounce the initial, medial vowel, and final sounds (phonemes) in three-phoneme (consonant-vowel-consonant, or CVC) words.* (This does not include CVCs ending with /l/, /r/, or /x/.) * Words, syllables, or phonemes written in /slashes/ refer to their pronunciation or phonology. Thus, /CVC/ is a word with three phonemes regardless of the number of letters in the spelling of the word.
RF.K.2e	Demonstrate understanding of spoken words, syllables, and sounds (phonemes). Add or substitute individual sounds (phonemes) in simple, one-syllable words to make new words.

RF.K.2f	Demonstrate understanding of spoken words, syllables, and sounds (phonemes). **Blend two to three phonemes into recognizable words. CA**

Phonics and Word Recognition

RF.K.3a	Know and apply grade-level phonics and word analysis skills in decoding words **both in isolation and in text. CA** Demonstrate basic knowledge of one-to-one letter-sound correspondences by producing the primary sounds or many of the most frequent sounds for each consonant.
RF.K.3b	Know and apply grade-level phonics and word analysis skills in decoding words **both in isolation and in text. CA** Associate the long and short sounds with common spellings (graphemes) for the five major vowels. **(Identify which letters represent the five major vowels [Aa, Ee, Ii, Oo, and Uu] and know the long and short sound of each vowel. More complex long vowel graphemes and spellings are targeted in the grade 1 phonics standards.) CA**
RF.K.3c	Know and apply grade-level phonics and word analysis skills in decoding words **both in isolation and in text. CA** Read common high-frequency words by sight (e.g., *the, of, to, you, she, my, is, are, do, does*).
RF.K.3d	Know and apply grade-level phonics and word analysis skills in decoding words **both in isolation and in text. CA** Distinguish between similarly spelled words by identifying the sounds of the letters that differ.

Fluency

RF.K.4	Read emergent-reader texts with purpose and understanding.

WRITING

Text Types and Purposes

W.K.1	Use a combination of drawing, dictating, and writing to compose opinion pieces in which they tell a reader the topic or the name of the book they are writing about and state an opinion or preference about the topic or book (e.g., *My favorite book is . . .*).
W.K.2	Use a combination of drawing, dictating, and writing to compose informative/explanatory texts in which they name what they are writing about and supply some information about the topic.
W.K.3	Use a combination of drawing, dictating, and writing to narrate a single event or several loosely linked events, tell about the events in the order in which they occurred, and provide a reaction to what happened.

Production and Distribution of Writing

W.K.4	(Begins in grade 2) CA
W.K.5	With guidance and support from adults, respond to questions and suggestions from peers and add details to strengthen writing as needed.

W.K.6	With guidance and support from adults, explore a variety of digital tools to produce and publish writing, including in collaboration with peers.
Research to Build and Present Knowledge	
W.K.7	Participate in shared research and writing projects (e.g., explore a number of books by a favorite author and express opinions about them).
W.K.8	With guidance and support from adults, recall information from experiences or gather information from provided sources to answer a question.
W.K.9	(Begins in grade 4)
Range of Writing	
W.K.10	(Begins in grade **2**) **CA**
SPEAKING AND LISTENING	
Comprehension and Collaboration	
SL.K.1a	Participate in collaborative conversations with diverse partners about *kindergarten topics and texts* with peers and adults in small and larger groups. Follow agreed-upon rules for discussions (e.g., listening to others and taking turns speaking about the topics and texts under discussion).
SL.K.1b	Participate in collaborative conversations with diverse partners about kindergarten topics and texts with peers and adults in small and larger groups. Continue a conversation through multiple exchanges.
SL.K.2a	Confirm understanding of a text read aloud or information presented orally or through other media by asking and answering questions about key details and requesting clarification if something is not understood. **Understand and follow one- and two-step oral directions. CA**
SL.K.3	Ask and answer questions in order to seek help, get information, or clarify something that is not understood.
Presentation of Knowledge and Ideas	
SL.K.4	Describe familiar people, places, things, and events and, with prompting and support, provide additional detail.
SL.K.5	Add drawings or other visual displays to descriptions as desired to provide additional detail.
SL.K.6	Speak audibly and express thoughts, feelings, and ideas clearly.
LANGUAGE	
Conventions of Standard English	
L.K.1a	Demonstrate command of the conventions of standard English grammar and usage when writing or speaking. Print many upper- and lowercase letters.

L.K.1b	Demonstrate command of the conventions of standard English grammar and usage when writing or speaking. Use frequently occurring nouns and verbs.
L.K.1c	Demonstrate command of the conventions of standard English grammar and usage when writing or speaking. Form regular plural nouns orally by adding /s/ or /es/ (e.g., *dog, dogs; wish, wishes*).
L.K.1d	Demonstrate command of the conventions of standard English grammar and usage when writing or speaking. Understand and use question words (interrogatives) (e.g., *who, what, where, when, why, how*).
L.K.1e	Demonstrate command of the conventions of standard English grammar and usage when writing or speaking. Use the most frequently occurring prepositions (e.g., *to, from, in, out, on, off, for, of, by, with*).
L.K.1f	Demonstrate command of the conventions of standard English grammar and usage when writing or speaking. Produce and expand complete sentences in shared language activities.
L.K.2a	Demonstrate command of the conventions of standard English capitalization, punctuation, and spelling when writing. Capitalize the first word in a sentence and the pronoun *I*.
L.K.2b	Demonstrate command of the conventions of standard English capitalization, punctuation, and spelling when writing. Recognize and name end punctuation.
L.K.2c	Demonstrate command of the conventions of standard English capitalization, punctuation, and spelling when writing. Write a letter or letters for most consonant and short-vowel sounds (phonemes).
L.K.2d	Demonstrate command of the conventions of standard English capitalization, punctuation, and spelling when writing. Spell simple words phonetically, drawing on knowledge of sound-letter relationships.
Knowledge of Language	
L.K.3	(Begins in grade 2)
Vocabulary Acquisitions and Use	
L.K.4a	Determine or clarify the meaning of unknown and multiple-meaning words and phrases based on *kindergarten reading and content*. Identify new meanings for familiar words and apply them accurately (e.g., knowing *duck* is a bird and learning the verb to *duck*).
L.K.4b	Determine or clarify the meaning of unknown and multiple-meaning words and phrases based on *kindergarten reading and content*. Use the most frequently occurring inflections and affixes (e.g., *-ed, -s, re-, un-, pre-, -ful, -less*) as a clue to the meaning of an unknown word.
L.K.5a	With guidance and support from adults, explore word relationships and nuances in word meanings. Sort common objects into categories (e.g., shapes, foods) to gain a sense of the concepts the categories represent.

L.K.5b	With guidance and support from adults, explore word relationships and nuances in word meanings. Demonstrate understanding of frequently occurring verbs and adjectives by relating them to their opposites (antonyms).
L.K.5c	With guidance and support from adults, explore word relationships and nuances in word meanings. Identify real-life connections between words and their use (e.g., note places at school that are *colorful*).
L.K.5d	With guidance and support from adults, explore word relationships and nuances in word meanings. Distinguish shades of meaning among verbs describing the same general action (e.g., *walk, march, strut, prance*) by acting out the meanings.
L.K.6	Use words and phrases acquired through conversations, reading and being read to, and responding to texts.

California English Language Development Standards

PART I: INTERACTING IN MEANINGFUL WAYS
A. COLLABORATIVE
1. Exchanging information and ideas
ELD.PI.K.1	**Emerging** Contribute to conversations and express ideas by asking and answering *yes-no* and *wh-* questions and responding using gestures, words, and simple phrases. **Expanding** Contribute to class, group, and partner discussions by listening attentively, following turn-taking rules, and asking and answering questions. **Bridging** Contribute to class, group, and partner discussions by listening attentively, following turn-taking rules, and asking and answering questions.
2. Interacting via written English
ELD.PI.K.2	**Emerging** Collaborate with the teacher and peers on joint composing projects of short informational and literary texts that include minimal writing (labeling with a few words), using technology where appropriate for publishing, graphics, etc. **Expanding** Collaborate with the teacher and peers on joint composing projects of informational and literary texts that include some writing (e.g., short sentences), using technology where appropriate for publishing, graphics, etc. **Bridging** Collaborate with the teacher and peers on joint composing projects of informational and literary texts that include a greater amount of writing (e.g., a very short story), using technology where appropriate for publishing, graphics, etc.

3. Offering opinions	
ELD.PI.K.3	**Emerging** Offer opinions and ideas in conversations using a small set of learned phrases (e.g., *I think X.*), as well as open responses. **Expanding** Offer opinions in conversations using an expanded set of learned phrases (e.g., *I think/don't think X. I agree with X.*), as well as open responses, in order to gain and/or hold the floor. **Bridging** Offer opinions in conversations using an expanded set of learned phrases (e.g., *I think/don't think X. I agree with X, but . . .*), as well as open responses, in order to gain and/or hold the floor or add information to an idea.
4. Adapting language choices	
ELD.PI.K.4	No standard for kindergarten.
B. INTERPRETIVE	
5. Listening actively	
ELD.PI.K.5	**Emerging** Demonstrate active listening to read-alouds and oral presentations by asking and answering *yes-no* and *wh-* questions with oral sentence frames and substantial prompting and support. **Expanding** Demonstrate active listening to read-alouds and oral presentations by asking and answering questions with oral sentence frames and occasional prompting and support. **Bridging** Demonstrate active listening to read-alouds and oral presentations by asking and answering detailed questions with minimal prompting and light support.
6. Reading/viewing closely	
ELD.PI.K.6	**Emerging** Describe ideas, phenomena (e.g., parts of a plant), and text elements (e.g., characters) based on understanding of a select set of grade-level texts and viewing of multimedia with substantial support. **Expanding** Describe ideas, phenomena (e.g., how butterflies eat), and text elements (e.g., setting, characters) in greater detail based on understanding of a variety of grade-level texts and viewing of multimedia with moderate support. **Bridging** Describe ideas, phenomena (e.g., insect metamorphosis), and text elements (e.g., major events, characters, setting) using key details based on understanding of a variety of grade-level texts and viewing of multimedia with light support.
7. Evaluating language choices	
ELD.PI.K.7	**Emerging** Describe the language an author uses to present an idea (e.g., the words and phrases used when a character is introduced) with prompting and substantial support. **Expanding** Describe the language an author uses to present an idea (e.g., the adjectives used to describe a character) with prompting and moderate support. **Bridging** Describe the language an author uses to present or support an idea (e.g., the vocabulary used to describe people and places) with prompting and light support.

8. Analyzing language choices	
ELD.PI.K.8	**Emerging** Distinguish how two different frequently used words (e.g., describing an action with the verb *walk* versus *run*) produce a different effect. **Expanding** Distinguish how two different words with similar meaning (e.g., describing an action as *walk* versus *march*) produce shades of meaning and a different effect. **Bridging** Distinguish how multiple different words with similar meaning (e.g., *walk, march, strut, prance*) produce shades of meaning and a different effect.
C. PRODUCTIVE	
9. Presenting	
ELD.PI.K.9	**Emerging** Plan and deliver very brief oral presentations (e.g., show and tell, describing a picture). **Expanding** Plan and deliver brief oral presentations on a variety of topics (e.g., show and tell, author's chair, recounting an experience, describing an animal). **Bridging** Plan and deliver longer oral presentations on a variety of topics in a variety of content areas (e.g., retelling a story, describing a science experiment).
10. Writing	
ELD.PI.K.10	**Emerging** Draw, dictate, and write to compose very short literary texts (e.g., story) and informational texts (e.g., a description of a dog), using familiar vocabulary collaboratively in shared language activities with an adult (e.g., joint construction of texts), with peers, and sometimes independently. **Expanding** Draw, dictate, and write to compose short literary texts (e.g., story) and informational texts (e.g., a description of dogs), collaboratively with an adult (e.g., joint construction of texts), with peers, and with increasing independence. **Bridging** Draw, dictate, and write to compose longer literary texts (e.g., story) and informational texts (e.g., an information report on dogs), collaboratively with an adult (e.g., joint construction of texts), with peers, and independently using appropriate text organization.
11. Supporting opinions	
ELD.PI.K.11	**Emerging** Offer opinions and provide good reasons (e.g., *My favorite book is X because X.*) referring to the text or to relevant background knowledge. **Expanding** Offer opinions and provide good reasons and some textual evidence or relevant background knowledge (e.g., paraphrased examples from text or knowledge of content). **Bridging** Offer opinions and provide good reasons with detailed textual evidence or relevant background knowledge (e.g., specific examples from text or knowledge of content).
12. Selecting language resources	
ELD.PI.K.12a	**Emerging** Retell texts and recount experiences using a select set of key words. **Expanding** Retell texts and recount experiences using complete sentences and key words. **Bridging** Retell texts and recount experiences using increasingly detailed complete sentences and key words.

ELD.PI.K.12b	**Emerging** Use a select number of general academic and domain-specific words to add detail (e.g., adding the word *spicy* to describe a favorite food, using the word *larva* when explaining insect metamorphosis) while speaking and composing. **Expanding** Use a growing number of general academic and domain-specific words in order to add detail or to create shades of meaning (e.g., using the word *scurry* versus *run*) while speaking and composing. **Bridging** Use a wide variety of general academic and domain-specific words, synonyms, antonyms, and non-literal language to create an effect (e.g., using the word *suddenly* to signal a change) or to create shades of meaning (e.g., The cat's fur was as *white as snow*.) while speaking and composing.

PART II: LEARNING ABOUT HOW ENGLISH WORKS

A. STRUCTURING COHESIVE TEXTS

1. Understanding text structure

ELD.PII.K.1	**Emerging** Apply understanding of how text types are organized (e.g., how a story is organized by a sequence of events) to comprehending and composing texts in shared language activities guided by the teacher, with peers, and sometimes independently. **Expanding** Apply understanding of how different text types are organized to express ideas (e.g., how a story is organized sequentially with predictable stages versus how an informative text is organized by topic and details) to comprehending texts and composing texts in shared language activities guided by the teacher, collaboratively with peers, and with increasing independence. **Bridging** Apply understanding of how different text types are organized predictably (e.g., a narrative text versus an informative text versus an opinion text) to comprehending texts and composing texts in shared language activities guided by the teacher, with peers, and independently.

2. Understanding cohesion

ELD.PII.K.2	**Emerging** Apply basic understanding of how ideas, events, or reasons are linked throughout a text using more everyday connecting words or phrases (e.g., *one time*, *then*) to comprehending texts and composing texts in shared language activities guided by the teacher, with peers, and sometimes independently. **Expanding** Apply understanding of how ideas, events, or reasons are linked throughout a text using a growing number of connecting words or phrases (e.g., *next, after a long time*) to comprehending texts and composing texts in shared language activities guided by the teacher, collaboratively with peers, and with increasing independence. **Bridging** Apply understanding of how ideas, events, or reasons are linked throughout a text using a variety of connecting words or phrases (e.g., *first/second/third, once, at the end*) to comprehending texts and composing texts in shared language activities guided by the teacher, with peers, and independently.

B. EXPANDING & ENRICHING IDEAS	
3. Using verbs and verb phrases	
ELD.PII.K.3a	**Emerging** Use frequently used verbs (e.g., go, eat, run) and verb types (e.g., doing, saying, being/having, thinking/feeling) in shared language activities guided by the teacher and with increasing independence. **Expanding** Use a growing number of verbs and verb types (e.g., doing, saying, being/having, thinking/feeling) in shared language activities guided by the teacher and independently. **Bridging** Use a wide variety of verbs and verb types (e.g., doing, saying, being/having, thinking/feeling) in shared language activities guided by the teacher and independently.
ELD.PII.K.3b	**Emerging** Use simple verb tenses appropriate for the text type and discipline to convey time (e.g., simple past for recounting an experience) in shared language activities guided by the teacher and with increasing independence. **Expanding** Use a growing number of verb tenses appropriate for the text type and discipline to convey time (e.g., simple past tense for retelling, simple present for a science description) in shared language activities guided by the teacher and independently. **Bridging** Use a wide variety of verb tenses appropriate for the text type and discipline to convey time (e.g., simple present for a science description, simple future to predict) in shared language activities guided by the teacher and independently.
4. Using nouns and noun phrases	
ELD.PII.K.4	**Emerging** Expand noun phrases in simple ways (e.g., adding a familiar adjective to describe a noun) in order to enrich the meaning of sentences and add details about ideas, people, things, etc., in shared language activities guided by the teacher and sometimes independently. **Expanding** Expand noun phrases in a growing number of ways (e.g., adding a newly learned adjective to a noun) in order to enrich the meaning of sentences and add details about ideas, people, things, etc., in shared language activities guided by the teacher and with increasing independence. **Bridging** Expand noun phrases in a wide variety of ways (e.g., adding a variety of adjectives to noun phrases) in order to enrich the meaning of phrases/sentences and add details about ideas, people, things, etc., in shared language activities guided by the teacher and independently.
5. Modifying to add details	
ELD.PII.K.5	**Emerging** Expand sentences with frequently used prepositional phrases (such as *in the house, on the boat*) to provide details (e.g., time, manner, place, cause) about a familiar activity or process in shared language activities guided by the teacher and sometimes independently. **Expanding** Expand sentences with prepositional phrases to provide details (e.g., time, manner, place, cause) about a familiar or new activity or process in shared language activities guided by the teacher and with increasing independence. **Bridging** Expand simple and compound sentences with prepositional phrases to provide details (e.g., time, manner, place, cause) in shared language activities guided by the teacher and independently.

C. CONNECTING & CONDENSING IDEAS	
6. Connecting ideas	
ELD.PII.K.6	**Emerging** Combine clauses in a few basic ways to make connections between and join ideas (e.g., creating compound sentences using *and*, *but*, *so*) in shared language activities guided by the teacher and sometimes independently.
	Expanding Combine clauses in an increasing variety of ways to make connections between and join ideas, for example, to express cause/effect (e.g., *She jumped because the dog barked.*) in shared language activities guided by the teacher and with increasing independence.
	Bridging Combine clauses in a wide variety of ways (e.g., rearranging complete simple sentences to form compound sentences) to make connections between and join ideas (e.g., *The boy was hungry. The boy ate a sandwich. -> The boy was hungry so he ate a sandwich.*) in shared language activities guided by the teacher and independently..
7. Condensing ideas	
ELD.PII.K.7	No standard for kindergarten.
Part III: Using Foundational Literacy Skills	
Foundational Literacy Skills	
ELD.PIII.K	Literacy in an Alphabetic Writing System • Print concepts • Phonological awareness • Phonics & word recognition • Fluency